Boombox

Also by Rupert M Loydell:

Poetry
An Experiment in Navigation (Shearsman Books, 2008)
Ex Catalogue (Shadow Train, 2006)
The Smallest Deaths (bluechrome, 2006)
A Conference of Voices (Shearsman Books, 2004)
Familiar Territory (bluechrome, 2004)
The Museum of Light (Arc Publications, 2003)
Home All Along (Chrysalis Poetry, 1999)

Collaborations
Memos to Self [with Nathan Thompson] (Underhand Behavior, 2009)
Overgrown Umbrellas [with Peter Dent] (Lost Property, 2008)
Risk Assessment [with Robert Sheppard] (Damaged Goods, 2006)
Make Poetry History [with Luke Kennard] (Miraculous Breath Books, 2006)
Shaker Room [with Lee Harwood] (Transignum, 2005)
Snowshoes Across the Clouds [with Robert Garlitz] (Stride, 2004)
Eight Excursions [with David Kennedy]
           (The Cherry On The Top Press, 2003)
The Temperature of Recall [with Sheila E. Murphy] (Trombone Press, 2002)
A Hawk into Everywhere [with Roselle Angwin] (Stride, 2001)

Rupert M Loydell

Boombox

Shearsman Books
Exeter

First published in the United Kingdom in 2009 by
Shearsman Books Ltd
58 Velwell Road
Exeter EX4 4LD

www.shearsman.com

ISBN 978-1-84861-058-3
First edition

Copyright © Rupert M Loydell, 2009.

The right of Rupert M Loydell to be identified as the author of this work has been asserted by him in accordance with the Copyrights, Designs and Patents Act of 1988. All rights reserved.

Acknowledgements:
Some of these poems have appeared in, or at,
Acumen, Approaching Rapture (Goldfish Fine Art), *Black Market Review, The Canting Academy* (IsPress), *The Construction of Memory* (Skylight Editions), *Envoi, Geometer, Gists & Piths, Great Works, Hummingbird,* LarryNorman.co.uk, LarryNorman.com, *Litter, Manifold, The Matthews House Project, Mimesis, Not Ichor, nthPosition, Only Connect* (Cinnamon Press), *Osiris, The Other Journal, Pages,* Penzance Poems in Windows Project – Golowan Festival 2007, *The PIP (Project for Innovative Poetry) blog, Poetry Scotland, Radix, Shadowtrain, Sphinx, Tears in the Fence, Temenos Academy Review, With, With+Stand.*

Cover painting 'Slab 3', copyright © Rupert Loydell, 2009

Contents

Safety Net

So Far Away	10
Hunger	12
Packing Up The Past	13
Safety Net	14
Cuckoo	15
Out of Sync	16
Tailspin	17
Mumble and Mutter	18
Cold Sunshine	19
Taking the Train	20
A Year Ago	21
The House with the Red Door	22
Roadworks	24

A Wing & A Prayer   25

The Unbelievable Truth

The Academy	42
Beyond the Stars	44
Blindsided	45
Boombox	46
A Cartoon Song	47
Cimabue	49
A Collection of Relics	50
Conviction	51
Disorienteering	52
Forgotten Outposts	53
Fugitive Scripting	54
A Glance is Enough: A Guide to Help Visitors	55
Going Under	57
Happy Ending	58
Held Together With Water	59
Inside Rain	60
Intermittent	61

The Map of Hearing	62
Memories for Amnesiacs	63
The Museum of Lists	64
Nearly Dry	66
Questions on Form	67
A Religion Concerning Essays	69
Running Away from the Clock	70
The Secret Life of the Artist	72
Some Things Just Happen	74
A Table of Moveable Feasts	75
The Unbelievable Truth	77
Understudy	78
What You Are, the World Is	79
When the Crowds Have Gone	80

Days for Amnesiacs

Days for Amnesiacs	84
Days for Amnesiacs 2	88
Days for Amnesiacs 3	90

October's Language

Strange Overtones	94
Up for Review	95
This is Where You End	97
Borrowed Time	99
How We Came to Be Where We Are	100
Stories All Around Us	101
Unwanted Visitors	102
A Few Thoughts About Blogging	104
Be Serious	106
The Last Word from Paradise	107
Do You Ever Get Lonely?	108
In Everything Give Thanks	110
Sources	111

for Jessica, Natasha and Sue.
Always.

> "I locked up all
> of the beautiful things
> that might move me."
> —Paige Ackerson-Kiely,
> 'The Potential of Rapture'

SAFETY NET

So Far Away

'Doesn't anybody stay in one place anymore?'
   — 'So Far Away', Carole King

Imagine there was a place
seven hours away by plane
with buildings pricking clouds
and jazz music in the park.

A place with bookshops
open till midnight and
books you want to read.

Slow flourish of sunrise
over skyscrapers: soon
we will be in New York.

•

Imagine there was a place
two hours away by train
where a muddy river washes
the edges of history and art.

A place I sing lovesongs for
and lived in as a child,
my half-forgotten city.

I am losing sight of whatever
growing up was, can no longer
say I belong in London.

•

Imagine there was a place
where our children felt safe
and the sunshine and sea
were never far away.

Imagine a place to call home
somewhere I didn't had to leave;
a little white room of my own.

There is. There was. I am
trying to localize the pain.
It hurts to move away.

Hunger

'My tummy is hungry now' says our daughter,
the morning after she has finished being sick.
Mine's full of curry and ache, indigestion
and worry, as we enter our final few days.
It is impossible to find things already packed,
difficult to relax or feel at ease. Outside
it's the second day of sunshine in a row.
The shed I have used for only one summer
is already warm inside but is piled high
with boxes and chairs. What on earth
are we going to do? This view of trees,
our struggling lawn, is going to haunt me,
this empty room always be filled
with poems and songs, overflowing shelves.
But now I am hungry for a new home,
somewhere where we can belong.

Packing Up The Past

Today, I hurriedly packed up my past
and took it to the dump. Tipped it
neatly out of the car and drove on.
Someone else can have it. I'm done
and dusted, off to somewhere else,
somewhere new. I can't control my
memories any more than the future,
but am doing my best to walk away
and forget the coming storm.
Everything is still to be decided.

On the way home from the doctor's
there are old men everywhere,
walking the pavements and alleys,
taking slow steps towards the future,
all carrying too much. I offer them
cardboard boxes so they can tidy
their secrets and worries away.
They tell me I will be sorry when
I get to their age and cannot recall
when nothing had been decided.

Safety Net

I shall look back on these years
as I looked through the pub window
yesterday: at a scene I'm no longer
part of. Who were all those people
I drank with? Why are they still there?
And how come only my life changed?

Now I won't have as much time for letters,
emails and drinks. Friendships that rely
on constant jostle and jibe of voice or text
won't last. Dialogue becomes monologue,
misty breath in the cold. I know it's warm
inside, know there's a safety net of company

I've fallen through, bruising myself on the way.

Cuckoo

'I'll find you one day raiding a brighter silence
or hugging the darker place you left for dead'
   — 'Containment', Peter Dent

Each morning the ship leaves harbour;
the past is here again.

In sunshine the village seems different:
acorns and oyster shells after the rain,

wet gardens and windblown leaves,
mudflats and mudlarks,

charred pumpkins and abandoned brooms,
smell of fireworks in the air.

I am on the isle of the dead,
a ghost among the living.

Friends moving too
share worries and wonders,

scars of recent removal.
I really don't want to go,

have lived here as long
as almost anywhere else.

Thank you for sending the image,
it looks like a still from a film.

Cuckoos in my nest delight.
Light ripples on the creek.

Out of Sync

'Summers make their own poems;
sometime you think that they haunt you.'
  — 'Summer Reflections', Harry Martinson

Sometimes the tide slips out of sync
with the way we live. Too late
to sail or row in the evenings—
it gets dark before the water arrives
and the pub is tempting and warm.

Sometimes the seasons slip out of sync
with the way we want to live. We end up
in the dark, reading *The Wishing Chair*
out loud and wondering where we could
go if only the world was as magical.

Sometimes our lives slip out of sync
and we are left all alone, looking at
a flattened and vanishing perspective,
nights interrupted by a 4 a.m. fox,
snout buried in the lawn, oblivious,

for sometimes time slips out of sync
with the way we are expected to live
and conduct ourselves in the suburbs:
we make our own poems and paper
over the cracks between granite slabs.

Sometimes everything slips out of sync.
A waxwing flies over the stone wall,
a branch drops from the oak tree,
the shadows hardly move. There is
no wind and no end to the moment.

TAILSPIN

All night in the village pub
the woman having a breakdown
spits out staccato questions

needing no answers.
Answers only lead to more questions.
Drink and questions keep flowing

as a policeman takes her away:
*What if*s and *Do you know*s and
*But*s and *Why*s suddenly gone . . .

In Em and Malcolm's garden
the birds spin song in the air,
flying from feeder to feeder.

They need nor give no answers
as I have my Full English Breakfast,
wondering at sanity and despair.

Mumble and Mutter

I am saying goodbye to the mumble and mutter
of Exeter cathedral, watching sunlight stream in
and colour the stone. Icons glow quietly,
carved figures in the wooden altarpiece frown.
Cathedral Yard is full of spring, just as it was
when we first moved here, though now
the High Street's lined with the same shops
you find everywhere else. It could be anywhere,
which is fortunate, because that is where
we are going. Paul and Graham are both
working today, so I get to say goodbye
and tell them our new address. This town
will simply become somewhere I used to live.
In my shed there is no wind, only tins of paint,
charity shop curtains, brushes, tools and rags.

There, I have happily mumbled and muttered
for many afternoons, making shelves or mending toys,
hidden from family and sun. I tried to explain
to my daughter how special places lose their magic,
how things fade and disappear. She's not convinced,
has only known this one town and her set of friends.
Seven years old and we are uprooting her;
even her baby sister knows the neighbours' names
and that we have packed her toys away. Will
our new house ever feel the same? Is there
enough room for our things? I hope spring
really is here, that the sun keeps shining down.
It's been a foggy winter, with hours spent on the road
and nights spent in a B&B. Now we must
rebuild our lives and try to make new friends.

Cold Sunshine

Warm baths and catnaps
while stomach cramps persist.

Only hot water does the trick
and allows me a little rest.

All night I've peeked
out at the river,

marking light's slow change
from dusk to dark to dawn.

At four a.m. the forced epiphany
of our windchimes in the mist.

By nine the horizon is back,
cold sunshine streaming in.

Taking the Train

Going back for the first time
since we moved, there's no reason
I know of to be scared but I am.
Months of commuting and worry
did me in—we nearly abandoned
the whole thing. I carried a sicknote
and resignation letter as a kind of
talisman as much as an escape plan.
I've only left the county once
since we arrived. Now autumn's here,
wind and endless rain. The beaches
are empty, we can visit Truro again;
even find somewhere to park. Cold
light shadows the flooded fields as I
paddle along the creek, marvelling at
my self-content. My new friend says
he's the same, lets people visit him,
though London still sometimes calls.
Back on the train, we pass a herd of
llamas who chew and stare. Hills of
waste have been turned green by time,
creepers climb old chimneys. Here
people live their lives, in secret places
we only catch a glimpse of going by.

A Year Ago

this place wasn't even on the radar
and we were looking for somewhere
to live. Didn't want to live in a village,
wasn't sure if I wanted the job.
Still aren't. But there was something
about the creek in the sunshine, the pub
and the people we met, how they talked
straightaway and told us their names,
recommended babysitters and schools.
Second time we were convinced, despite
the swirly carpets and nasty textured walls.
Most of that's gone now, we're slowly
getting sorted. It's difficult to remember
what went before, the view from other
windows. Here, the mist is burning off
the hills, birds gather at the feeders
in the garden. A year ago, we didn't know
this place existed. Now it feels like home.

The House with the Red Door
for Jessica, who asked

Can we go back to the house with the red door?
We must disregard old favourites, learn to forget
the past. It is usually found where there is not
too much direct sunlight, a sudden picture that
was hidden but is still included. No-one was able
to write down things exactly as they happened
but images are preserved with amazing sharpness.

We are surprised by the apparition, the sound
of a wind-up toy in motion, the bustle of mind
in the mouth. It is a time for our words to dance
and our bodies to celebrate spring, time to convince
the children they don't really miss their last home.
We concentrate on the positive: larger garden, safe
places to cycle, their treehouse, how near the village

is to the creek. Some days we canoe in the rain,
disturbing herons and geese, but when the sun shines
we paddle along to the pub and think how lucky we are.
There is nothing unexpected about these events, except
that they are new, and almost justify moving. What is
the point of this small landscape we have adopted
unless we can call it home? It is a different space

to the city, with different meanings for words like
distance and proximity. This is the pub, that is
the church, and there is the village hall. The shop
is a mile in that direction, if you want to moor
your boat here talk to Pete. It's nice in the bar
when the tourists go home, though it's their meals
that fund our quiet drinks. Whatever point of access

takes the mood or imagination, there are only
two roads in, the lane with passing places out.
A chasm has been opened and this is where
I want my poem to go, rowing across the sky
of water at high tide. We cannot ever go back
through the red door. It is no longer our house,
we would not recognize it as even the same world.

Roadworks

Eight o'clock on a Monday morning and
workmen are busy moving the portaloo
to somewhere nearer; then it will be time
for a pot of tea. It's all go! Good-looking
women in oversized cars scowl through
their windscreens. Why is the lane
closed off for so long? There is no sign
of improvement, just an endless diversion.

On the way to work my car stalls again:
lights flicker and the engine dies. It
coughs back into life straightaway, but
meanwhile the queue heckles and hoots.
I am so easily embarrassed, try hard
not to panic or rush. Breathe deep,
stay calm, and gently turn the key.
My life is an endless diversion.

A Wing & A Prayer

interludes, interventions and interpretations

"I want to make images that have open,
narrative qualities, enough to suggest
ideas about human limits."
—Robert Parke Harrison

"There is a tradition [. . .] that the first
man to wake each morning must sweep
shadows from his porch lest night
pull the long limbs of sunlight
into its mouth and devour the day."
—Bob Hicok, 'Translator's Note'

"—and now let us ride off on the vehicle of language"
—Gerhard Roth, *The Autobiography of Albert Einstein*

For Will Menter and Richard Skelton,
who made the pictures in sound,

and Kodo,
who first showed me Robert ParkeHarrison's photos.

Whatever strings I can find to pull
I'll pull, then take cover behind
cold walls in other cities where

I will short-circuit inspiration
and begin to write a sequence
of lunatic ballads and songs,

imagine low-voltage characters,
compose a symphony
of catcalls and natural speech.

Shadowed days pass by,
re-imagined as a circus
peopled by frowning clowns

with high-wire performance stories:
the slow-turning wheel of a monocycle
above a safety net full of flowers.

Digital manipulation relates
directly to the picture space,
absence re-emerging in new

and surprising configurations,
a glimpse of something wonderful:
people in the dark watching people

in the dark, snagged moments
attacked and captured, then
exposed to the force of time.

•

There is something about this strange space
that will keep us together. The phrase *apt
and dubious* is not especially apt nor dubious.

There is something about falling in dreams
that makes me want to wake up. This time
I have brought along furniture for company:

chairs and tables, cats and dog, an umbrella
in case it rains. The world seems a long way
down, the sky is so high above. There is

something about undefined space that is
both alarming and strange. I cannot reach
the proffered hand or the book of birds.

The next frame is a clean slate. When I
am gone it will be better late; think of me
then and use me perhaps as a paperweight.

•

Fugitive pieces of the pirate's gospel:
transient life in the twilight, a hang-
over jig around buckets of optimism
and a small circle of neglected saplings.

All I ever wanted was to run to the ghost
and remember how clouds collapsed
as my mirror spoke. This is no reflection
on you, it is simply the mirrorball light

in the wounded wood one morning
in spring. On a day like this, showers
cause the sky to collapse and blood
to run downhill. A storm is coming

and it is not the weather to fly. My friend
is late, it is like waiting for the testcard
to move across the television screen.
Every forest has its shadow: this is mine.

•

Scaffold the planet and climb to the top,
make like a revolution, dance a rain dance
to keep warm and dry. Plant dry twigs
and wait for sleep to raise me to the sky.

I hitchhike a ride to the nearest star,
can always be distracted by experiment.
Breathe in the air and exhale water, spit
into the pail. Rinse and smile, light up

a cigarette, stick opinion in your eye. My
precarious perch is a rod for my own back;
further along the airways, others sleep and
wait for instructions, imaginary flight plans.

Swinging from a homemade trapeze,
I circle the earth and scratch the surface.
God would not leave me hanging here;
he is the navigator, not me. All in all,

you are on my radar and off the map.
Windmaker, I am blown about
and all confused. Ascension is
a flying device, a spiritual journey

with birds and gears and empty pots,
string and withies, hope. A wing
and a prayer does not describe how
my life proceeds from this point on.

I jot all the details down as the storm
proceeds in an orderly manner from
front to front to front. Ready or not,
I am cleared for take off. Watch me go.

•

The flying machine fills our house
with glass and glitter, foil and string.

In the cold shadow of the dark sun
garden wire drones in the wind,

dust coils on paving stones
as the dream switch is thrown.

Broken home ghost hardware
is written over in a moment

(manifest spirit infestation,
plucked danger zone infill),

the burnt white ink ascending
to this nothing already then.

•

Cloudburst infiltration and flooded memory,
river sleep and boxes of dreams piled high.
I am chaining myself to the past and
ignoring the marks we made. The future
is above the clouds; I loose the birds
and tame the sky, pedal faster toward
the distant light. But bells of memory
weigh me down and I remain seated
on stone. I'll still be here in the morning,

dreaming of crows and empty cages,
an electric fan in perpetual motion
blowing us all to where we should be.
Listen, you can hear the wind sing
and clouds crying, the sound of men
inside a shut book of small pictures
and pale tones wanting to fly,
the sound of an exhausted globe
sighing in silvered slow motion.

•

In the garden of self
there are lights in the distance,

riddles and fairytales,
a sunlit clearing in the woods

a sprawl of people
as the heavens open up.

Sing chords of resonance
in a dark and difficult language,

stand on the last star
and don't look down.

Fall out of reach,
sky dive into the space between.

•

The moon's a real cliché grin
looking down on me tonight.
Orion's belt glints, the estuary birds

call; I'm so glad I live where I do.
Middle class malaise, quiet streets,
friendly village; another attempt
to fly away from here to the light.

•

It takes a pair of artists to start building
their own pipe dreams, galleries and space,
make this mixture of magic and disarray.

Progressive brain disease meant
earth and driftwood and pottery
sheltered them from the elements.

Robbed of the ability to speak or think,
they needed a beautiful place to live;
the compound is bounded by a creek.

If waters are low you can wade across,
otherwise go to the bathhouse,
where the shower is a length of hose

and the windows are stained glass.
A non-existent floor plan shows more
than a hectare of fantastic domes,

hidden shacks and follies. Seems they'd
never done anything to nurture the arts,
stayed always, always, on the other side.

•

Piece by piece,
artists' hands
made this home.

Anarchy rules,
music is loud,
dishes stay dirty.

The camp
is a symbol
of hope and despair,

the residents
have learnt
to keep quiet.

That assertion
is misleading
at least,

at most
is a flight
from language

into words,
which is how
each summer day begins.

•

On the other side of the pond
lives a man who plays with bits
of wood. And when I say plays,
I mean in the musical sense.

He rescues songs from the forest;
instruments from the natural dam,
the undergrowth, the stream;
notes from out of the woodpile.

String a line and sing a song,
then listen. Each thonk echoes
and echoed clunk dances
along the string, the wire,

echoes and falls, reverberates.
What does sound look like?
A pile of sticks, a windchime,
branches blowing in the wind.

•

He made props
and found time
to arrange them,
dressed the part
and got ready to
fly to the clouds
on a ladder,
tame and catch
raw lightning,
cycle into eternity,
take another photo.

•

The rediscovery of the xylophone
occurred when the ladder fell apart
and he arranged the rescued rungs
by weight and broken length.

It was impossible to talk because
of the way noise filled his head.
Sound would have to live elsewhere,
with people who listened out loud.

In the viewfinder, silver flashbulbs
synchronised with secondhand light.
He burned the wood to keep him warm
and made a picture book to remember,

hung it from the branches of his mind,
watched as dancers and children played,
collected leaves and music for themselves,
each moment touching all his memories.

•

Personal space
in a virtual realm

makes some people
more likely to cheat.

In digital self-expression
it is the girls who rule.

Geeky males are uneasy
about what the future may bring.

A homeland is so hard to find.

•

I keep my books on my shelves,
my shelves in my fields.
I keep my land in order.

I keep myself to myself,
file and burn my memories.
My metabolism often fails:

my heartbeat is a bell
that chimes on the hour,
my days are long and slow.

I watch your lips move
and mime my understanding;
my hearing is not what it was.

Watch my lips move
as language drags me along.
My speech is a rusty plough.

After all my comings and goings
I have arrived here.
This is where I shall stay.

I bury my books and letters,
keep only photographs of words.
Ideas form in dangerous ways.

•

Are you two people? I am diverse,
artificially illuminated and half alive,
a phantom of spotlight and neon.

This passage through silence and light
takes you to the bunker,
a concrete ruin half-buried in the sea.

Each night I glow with expectation
and the fallout of the past.
My hands are the texture of sand,

my eyes see past you to flooded fields
and on towards the scribbled horizon.
On the beach, bleached driftwood at dawn.

I shiver in the imaginary wind.

•

Fictional mechanics and staged events
are unlikely to fool the participants
or cure our feverish dreams.

Awkwardness and ineptitude means
you're more likely to sink than swim.
Torn landscapes repeatedly exposed

look old and worn, dark and lifeless.
What we're seeing is cultural history
ultimately lifted by unflagging belief.

The black-suited character is everyone,
is always on the lookout for land uglier
than his own. The maker defies gravity,

becomes a blip on the radar. There are
messages coming in from the architect,
he is planting fresh sentences as we speak,

although they may turn out to be somebody
speaking like a human being about being
a human being, or rather singing like one.

•

Jack and Jill flew up the hill
weighed down by pails of water.
Surely, they'll need more
than brown paper rhymes,
when the wings fall off
and their plane comes down?

Stick men and cloud machines,
another failed attempt to fly.
I risk the ultimate high dive,
trespass in the sunshine and
recall your final hospitalization.
There is so much I want to know.

Today I wrote nothing, no words
flew between us. Death is easy,
if you go too far you will see
what it is impossible to forget.
Spill out names, warm blood
and regret, all I need to know.

•

Secret notebooks, wild pages;
broken wings, discarded feathers.
I don't want my work to be about me.

What would it look like
if there was a hole in the sky?
Stainless steel droppings and stars.

It feels like I'm stumbling in the dark
with both my hands outstretched.
I don't want my work to be about me.

If electricity hadn't been invented,
how would you make light?
I would try to capture the moon.

Oversized objects, improbable acts;
lucid dreaming, organized effects.
I don't want my work to be about me.

•

Camouflage masters turn hidden faces
to the sun. Big oaks sway, the rain falls
until we meet again. A prayer becomes
a flower; the slow life is gaining devotees
who have created self-organizing systems:

a denim scarecrow in the wind, broken
conversation in the clouds, nuclear skies,
turquoise light, stars in resurrection night.
No one is left in the lightning tree, only
scared crows remain in the dented mind.

The Unbelievable Truth

The Academy

Ah, these Academy boys are ambitious! The Academy is an all-year-round scheme where students are given important tools and are selected. The freshness of life is not about modern-day peasants with shiny building blocks but the primary need to prioritise stellar evolution. Life is about to teach these kids a lesson for the ages: these guys must do the dishes and their armpits. Minor changes have not compromised the overall design or the date of their death. Academy boys are to be kept Academy boys.

High personal standards and self-motivation are essential. These are basic truths that no one can argue with, truths which are the cornerstone for building and developing conscientious, reliable citizens for the future. Each day we challenge ourselves to embrace all the children in our society. This exercise is important for overall stability and strength, and provides a structured and disciplined alternative to parents who have come to the end. Our mission is to pursue, encourage and maintain excellence in the field and to promote advances and campaigns.

At the minute we're stretched a little bit because a lot of the Academy boys are in the Reserves. Their absence produces positive peer pressure and negative behavior. While I feel very sorry for these boys, rules are rules, full of contradictions, flat-out lies and groundless affirmations. If you have any questions, we recommend that you get the nod. Do not hesitate, use one of these and one of those. Please contact the registrar if you would like to learn more.

The Academy is recognized nationally as an educational resource center, a learning, sharing, mentoring, networking, benchmarking and empowering institution that evolves continuously. The Academy brings students face-to-face with the extraordinary leaders, thinkers and pioneers who have shaped our world, and has the largest single malt collection in old Brunswick. This leads to development and acceleration of giftedness in gifted children with accelerated learning.

The Academy can only reflect the official discourses of the day. You and your family are encouraged to tour any time of the year and encounter the professor who is totally disengaged. Medieval numbskulls cannot guarantee top marks. Give trouble a second chance, spread rumours in your own time and under these conditions the Academy is permanently shut down. We're absolutely delighted, and would like to thank God and the Academy for making possible everything we've achieved.

Beyond the Stars
i.m. Larry Norman

A celebration. Projected memories
and the sound of a scratched record,
the descent of the first man, Adam,
as song echoes against the casket.
Find the fragile path into the future
and wait for me beyond the stars.

Today I wrote nothing. There will be
no more words flying between us,
nothing developed as a metaphor.
Death is as easy as lying, as rumour
spread against you, around you,
stories you pretended not to hear.

At the limit of translation, you
reinvented the wheel. Practice
can be observed, evaluated;
what you did cannot. Take
that fragile path into eternity
and wait beyond the stars.

Today I wrote something. This
is not an obituary or a memorial,
nothing here feels deliberate
or right. In another future,
where you are fit and well,
we see you in a new light

and understand love's defiance.

Blindsided

It is dark in the luminarium. There is
just enough light to see how the moon
hangs by a thread from the rafters.

The bats are happiest. And the owls
who are lost in sunshine and at night:
ghost birds on the towers of silence.

With moth wings and antennae
we might feel our way to morning;
frightened fingers flick the unseen.

Fear is a slow death-march to nowhere
alongside steam-trains rusting in the dark.
Our lunatic captive illuminates memory

but we have forgotten what we do not know.
The past is about to explode from the centre
and we are no use now if we cannot speak.

Boombox
for Anthony

Frosted colour and splashback.
Windows as high as the ceiling
and doors to private worlds

where radios on timers
tame and catch the music
as it falls upon Penzance.

The boombox can't keep up.
All this zigzag electricity
amplifies the sound,

and these canvasses
are way too small for
what you want to paint.

It is as easy as singing
and alters the neural
connections in the brain,

is a rapid short circuit
of chaos, an equation
of movement and line,

is as natural as falling
into friendship, as hard
as grey concrete walls.

We cannot get a word in
and would not want to:
you are so noisily alive.

A Cartoon Song
for Peter Gillies

My friend who paints pictures quickly
and considers every word he writes
is worried about freedom. This essay,
he says, is undefined, brings a new
set of problems to the course.
In the pub, Bill seizes upon
the catalogue of paintings I've
brought along as if it's magic,
and can see it all straightaway.

Work I've struggled to comprehend
he glances at and understands. In
Guinness terms it's all fluid dynamics
and computer hum, the chaotic crackle
of life today: interference and inter-
ruption, the way we circle around
common occurrences, the sudden
slash and slide of colour within a
black outline or bright pattern box.

All things to all: overwritten poems
and under-rehearsed excuses,
moments of wonder and confusion.
The CD skips in the jukebox to make
the best dance loop I've ever heard.
'Time to go home gentlemen.'
And for once the landlord is right.
Wonder goes back in the plastic bag,
we neck what's left in the glass and

head out into the dark. Things that
float, things that live, things that die
are on show in a gallery nearby.
The world is in the making and
all my marking waits to be done.
If we could slow down or just not
speed up, this would be a cartoon
song. As it is, it's a long way from
here to where we started out, so

I'd best be moving on. The artist
emailed back and said he'd send
a catalogue but the gallery never
replied. Life is by invitation only,
we are all natural and legitimate
heirs. You have always been intent
upon challenging how the poem
might be made, but I am beginning
not to care. Intuition seems to do.

CIMABUE

Memory makes a noise
like paint peeling,
dark flood water
falling away.

Death by drowning:
the ruined crucifix
still floats in imagination,
resurrected and restored.

Flakes of reverence
and moments of dusk;
everything in Italy
is a love letter to God.

A Collection of Relics

Tap the seconds slowly.
Chin in the wrong hand,
I remember

staring at the same window,
a damaged photo,
cold wood floor.

Scuff and swirl of light,
cracked and broken glass,
lost focus.

A furious child shakes a tall weed,
waits for the sun to move
before a goodnight kiss.

Private references & stage-managed figures:
the projection of personal terrors,
this collection of relics.

The tender elegance of death
in pathological reproductions;
indifference is a creed.

Hurrah for America
and the prone man,
the log jam.

Hurrah for
counting lessons in purgatory,
life spread-eagled on the rock.

CONVICTION

Come and listen to our song.
The whole is a shadow,

like listening in on something
when you're not supposed to,

drawn in by the weave
of incidental fragments.

Overwhelming moments of bliss
leave me light-headed, lethargic.

Say no again to the broken heart:
it's never felt so magnificent to be lost.

Disorienteering

The visitors are still here,
making holes in the timetable,
pauses in the playback.

The days are awry:
someone's in the bathroom
and talking on the phone,

the television is up too loud
and on the wrong channel,
there's nowhere for me to work.

Our vegetables are undercooked
and the kitchen is not clean.
I didn't want a curry anyway.

It's a circle-house experience
where space is at a premium
and I want to hide away,

it is time for disorienteering,
time to put my mind in the trees
and be who I do not want to be.

Forgotten Outposts

'the sound in my life enlarges my prison'
  —Tom Phillips

Music is important for many reasons
but I have forgotten what they are.

For years, resonance couldn't be captured
and song was lost in the mists of time.

Now, I desire to capture the moth,
create works based on a set of rules.

My message is that even mundane events
are to be cherished, all sounds are unique:

the chatter of fax machines, the drip of water,
footsteps, rustling leaves and gentle rain

are all as valuable as any instrument.
Listening frames texture and emotion

in a sunlit mix of abstract warmth:
newspaper stories and family events,

blurred polaroids of remaindered moments,
time past confined to rows of dotted lines.

'I don't really believe in a visual language,
composition is determined by the thing itself.'

FUGITIVE SCRIPTING
for Iain Sinclair

A transient passage through night haunts
and unstable information networks, dreaming
of thrown-away guidebooks and multiple selves.
The world is water, gobbets of autobiography
multi-channelled through the new century.

Trauma narratives are often politics
from another angle. Few hanker after
property investment or hold out for culture;
many inhabit discordant imagination,
ice-age architecture of their own design.

My favourite animal is full of despair
and unacknowledged magnetism. Conspiracy
is problematic in terms of truth: consider
the play of shadow and light at the margins
as the finished book enters the bloodstream.

A Glance is Enough: A Guide to Help Visitors
for Bob Garlitz

Begin with a good long look. Silence is the means to worship, so open this notebook and write down half a page at the very least. Have fun with a variety of activities, then stop and look ahead.

What do you see? An interview, a semi-realist form, a tremendous amount of dark power. Blunt guesses at truth.

What do these colours make you think of? A child who sits under tables and in cupboards, annoyed by everything it fails to understand.

What keeps the stripe fascinating? How rare and outwardly uniform they are. Reading them, we understand the effort of will involved in sustaining the still surface.

How would you describe these stripes? A noisy rhetoric receiving widespread recognition, a scar left on water, air and earth. They burn like stars and draw people like a magnet.

What is different about these stripes? Something has been opened up, let in. They oscillate between language and flesh, are centred around detailed observation.

Do you feel a connection? No. Elm or maple offers better shade. I sit still, trying not to move. The eyes' rapid movement fixes objects in vision, and the mind eschews the pre-existing form. Prayer has a similar effect.

A door into what? Floating thoughts and dreams, the silencing of self and will. I like the idea of mirroring feeling. The sphere resembles a pumpkin in the chaos of the world.

What surrounds the door? A strange mixture of cultural homogeneity and exuberant invention, a developed field of workshop techniques involving meditation, repetition and self-discipline.

What kind of dialogue is happening? Texts confront our inner desire to interpret head on; the unspoken life must be made to speak up, like the spaces between slabs and blocks.

Is there a search for something? There is. The story that is always almost but not quite present has become its own cultural mediator.

If so, what? Ultimately, revelation: how does one's voice become bigger than oneself? How does one's vision come to be representative in a world of momentary engagement?

Explore the drama, but stare love down. Stay out of my way, and close the door behind you when you leave. Observe art from a safe distance.

Going Under

Across an endless field of monochrome,
angels stomp and forget what is unfinished.

Theirs is a perfect neglect, an accidental memory
of earth, where hymns are a prelude to death

and shivering human beings confuse the theory
of machines with schools of emotional engineering.

Hammer the halo and wait for the good times
to be announced. I see through you, can't stay.

Baby, nobody's perfect, but I am wiping out.
Forgetting you will be like breathing water.

Happy Ending

Somewhere, somebody else is doing what I have done.
Singing on the beach in a moment of transcendence
or discovering they are a dad. Someone has probably
canoed up the creek and discovered my special place.
We are not as unique as we seem or would like and
everything that happens is not here in my poems.

Follow the diversion and make of it what you will.
Somebody else is in charge now and they write all
the rules. Early morning starts reduce me to a fool
who bumbles and clatters around the house before
collapsing into the car. Later, strong coffee revives
and I can make enough sense to be going on with.

All our past is unspoken—only sometimes do we
give it voice. Everyday occurrences they may be
but how often memories still hurt. The days stretch
back and forwards, the children always grow older.
I never get to the studio now, have forgotten how
to paint. It is always going to be once upon a time.

Held Together With Water
for Alan

My daughter is having a panic attack, midstream,
as her kayak floats away. The wind and the tide
are pushing her where she doesn't want to be
now the sunshine for our picnic has gone.

I got lost in a box of Lego with the girl next door.
When I am older I want a puppy but the way
will be blocked by rows of raspberry bushes
and angry swans. There are gliders overhead,

guardian angels trying to catch the wind. A table,
adrift in the river, is inches deep in dust. I cut
my finger on the wooden gate when I got home.
"Call me that again and I will break your nose."

Death called me on my mobile to let me know that
you had fallen off the balcony into intensive care.
The bleeding has stopped but you're still sedated
while student heartache goes on. This is the week

for final submissions, you're less pale than before.
We number hurt in sequence as memory pulls apart,
and protect ourselves from damage, dust and wear.
Held together with water, I pull the boat to shore.

Inside Rain

He found it hard to cope with,
autumn already being here. And
it was Friday. Next week at work,
students would arrive, days blur
into photocopying and lectures.

Summer? What summer? Outside,
rain was falling, fields were on fire.
He smouldered with impatience,
tried to find time to make time to
do the things he should have done

when he'd had the time. A week ago
he thought he'd relaxed, been glad
to be; now the sun set earlier and
earlier, and every resolution failed.
How he feared the days to come,

misunderstood the principle of night
and day, couldn't see how it slotted
all together. Later on, he watched
the rain, the visiting foxes and owls,
wondered about money, light, and love.

INTERMITTENT

History never changes, we just peg our clothes up
in a different order, depending on the wind and sun.
Intermittent reality is all you will ever know, so just
underline the truth in red, mark it secret, file it away—
but spare yourselves the details: throw these words out now.
Plant out the future and water well, see what morning brings;
when and how high the tide is, how fast the traffic flows.
Sometimes life is at a standstill and I hear the sound
of ghosts long dead, the kids playing in the kitchen.
Listen, listen, listen children: history changes everything.

We crash its gears and drive away too fast, talking over
those who interrupt. We'll sing and shout or scream
for as long as it takes to win. Superimpose the future
if you want, it doesn't change the way things are. You
couldn't make it up, what has happened to me or what
lies up ahead. It's my story, my word against theirs—
all I have are half-truths and lies with consequences
still to come. Every road has a silver lining, each cloud
drops snow and rain. These are the only secrets I know
when I'm out and about or am too late coming home.

History's made up of secondhand stories ironed into shape
then put away in drawers where no-one can find them.
Books arrive unasked for from people I don't know
who think it might be important for me to have a say.
I spare myself the pleasure and give them all away.
You can download the future now, or deduce it from
the shape of the skull and how the body lies. Nobody
around here knows me and that's the way it should be.
I want to be a man out in his boat, a stranger at the bar;
am not the least bit frightened of history having its say.

The Map of Hearing

Was it the hum of the printer
or music he could hear?

Nothing had changed except
his relationship to the room

and noise that seemed
to come from nowhere.

Cabin fever, perhaps, or
signals from outer space,

the house full of tones,
unabridged equations and

out-of-balance sound,
broken wires scrawled

across the map of hearing.

Memories for Amnesiacs

I like being told what to do,
the music I should be listening to.

One student knows far more than I
and is glad to voice his opinion,

another wants to reinvent hip-hop
and give up smoking without any pain.

Fantastic voyages are to be had
by intentionally going nowhere:

I can fold time and space,
be whoever I want to be.

Frontiers and countries keep moving
without warning, walls keep tumbling

down. My daughter's favourite phrase
is 'when I was a baby I used to . . .'

She invents a past she can't remember,
paints pictures to hang on memory's wall.

The Museum of Lists
for Dean Young

the metal museum: the circulation of signs
the museum of biscuits: the elemental state of materials
the wax museum: tonight we sleep with the long dead king
the museum of retrotechnology: the hot tub was not meant to be used
the museum of breakfast: mouths open, teeth showing
the museum of childhood: the cry at zero
the museum of witchcraft: abstract frottages depicting psychic energy
the online museum: a black hole in which logic meets indecision
the museum of power: firing at random into the crowd
the transport museum: a man on the sidewalk with a mechanical leg
the museum of advertising: the language of capitalism
the museum of fruit: a last slip of orange above the ridge
the wool museum: creature comforts and the easy life
the museum of brewing: an unquenchable thirst to discover
the museum of everything: visible quirks and hidden tragedies
the museum of spam: the outcome of digital technology's onslaught
the museum of myth and fable: a work in progress
the museum of firepower: unconstrained access to lethal weaponry
the museum of broken relationships: nothing to be upset about
the police museum: a framed official document
the museum of pure form: the loudness of sine waves
the yo-yo museum: relaunched as a spiritual exercise
the boomerang museum: a strictly enforced policy of no re-admittance
the museum of bacteria: viral spread and a sense of obligation
the museum of burnt food: a chronicle of disaster
the museum of lost interactions: the transparency of documentation
the museum of the moving image: a flight of steps for chorus girls to
      descend
the textile museum: ellipses of colorful yarn occupy the space
the museum of tattoos: an arresting array of bloody red stains
the museum of broken packets: notice the holes
the museum of bad art: doomed to be taken all too literally
the museum of flight: shore leave ornithology
the museum of electricity: the bright light of the mind

the museum of unnatural mystery: fails to reflect anything clearly
the museum of reconstruction: vague ideas of replication
the museum of failure: under the bed some pieces of broken glass
the museum of unworkable devices: a text about the world right now
the museum of earth: an oath between trees and rocks
the museum of hoaxes: staging the narrative
the museum of funeral customs: the approaching fate of customers

Nearly Dry

The dialect lines across europe stream
down to the sea through fields of dots
unlike anything except spattered paint
or dust in your eye.

It is good to hear the seesaw of gossip
and see tables set out on the verge.
We want a well run pub, never mind
a beer festival.

You led us up to where the paintings
lay ready for sale: silvers and greys,
creams and soft whites, seductively
saying it right.

The studio was a simple wooden shed.
We tiptoed around the trampoline,
ignoring the binaries which always
let us down.

A fat ginger cat followed us into spring
where my workload increases and time
fills up whilst colour calls from un–
finished work.

Rum and beer. When he finally woke up
we were back from our camping trip and
everything was Bank Holiday. We'd wanted
to go to the beach.

Outside the sun is shining and the tent
is draped over the car. Please take me to
wherever it is that armchairs go to die.
Everything is nearly dry.

Questions on Form
for Luke

You are offered a drink by a good looking man in a bar.
Do you
(a) take the dog for a walk?
(b) join alcoholics anonymous?
(c) start again from the beginning?

You are a good looking man in a bar, offering a drink to a stranger.
Do you
(a) weave an allegory out of the word 'offer'?
(b) get lost in the beard of wisdom?
(c) adopt a different attitude?

You are drinking heavily at the bar.
Do you
(a) bear your pain and misery?
(b) run for cover?
(c) recognise ambiguity as another form of meaning?

You are unable to get home from the pub as you have spent all your money.
Do you
(a) emphasise lines, spaces, constructions?
(b) turn the volume up?
(c) cut shapes out of time?

You are hungover in a deserted ballroom.
Do you
(a) obsess about the music of the past?
(b) hark back to the misty moonlight?
(c) stir your pot of words?

You are dogged by the photographic visual.
Do you
(a) go among words?
(b) look for a bare room?
(c) continue to probe the aesthetic?

You are indifferent to good and evil.
Do you
(a) offer a slap to the face of moral hypocrisy?
(b) celebrate the power of documentary?
(c) formulate a credo ?

You rebuff the conventions of ordinary knowledge.
Do you
(a) take a pessimistic view of the future?
(b) contaminate meaning?
(c) go out for a drink?

You cannot be trusted, can you?
In the final scene, imagination
plays fast and loose with itself,
uncertainty pervades the text,
and everything else vanishes.

A Religion Concerning Essays
for John Burnside

'Cuz there will come a time
When time goes out the window
And you'll learn to drive out of focus.'
   — 'Going Inside', John Frusciante

Off to a great start, almost godlike in fact—
moments of understanding in need of enlargement.
I have been spared any camaraderie of loneliness
and now understand what I am expected to do.

Faint horizontal lines in pencil, footnotes and asides;
declared intention and clear evidence of thought.
Truth matters, according to the book I am reading.
I don't know if that is true or just a construct.

From a distance, knowledge is a good and constant
sort of companion. Love is mentioned just the once,
faith only in passing; in the future we will not see at all.
I put doubt in my pocket and take it across town.

For punctuation there are footsteps, car horns, mobile phones,
barking dogs, strange voices off and disconnected speech.
'I love colour more than anything else!" she is still wont
to exclaim. We all thank Providence for deliverance

but this is soon matched by fears of critical discernment:
those wretched academics have a lot to answer for.
There is no excuse for not wearing my glasses, none
for leaving the road. This trip is an artistic pilgrimage,

the assignment merely a ruse to see if you were listening.
When was that deadline again? Rightly or wrongly,
we are all in this together, nothing less than human,
spilling into self-absorption and superstitious ways.

Running Away from the Clock
for Alan West

>   'You wouldn't
> like it here. Go elsewhere. One person's
> Torrola is another's Sadness-by-the-Sea.'
>   —Stephen Dunn, 'Postcard from Torrola'

Diaries of forgotten happiness,
photographs of the past,
offer presences and dimensions.

Strange world. Because of me
rivers burn and run backwards
shaping our unconscious.

My body is a landscape
of social realities and carbon footprints.
Breathe in the beautiful smog.

Distant relations are my inheritance,
tomorrow's forecast is strikingly clear:
a collaborative elegy until we meet again.

Hundred-year-old trees are in bloom.
Don't give up the ghost, the life or work,
try and stay under the influence.

New galaxies form like droplets,
mirror universe pulls back the shade
(enjambment from heat to sub-zero).

Nomad words, spiral lands:
an oath between trees & rocks,
empires and environments,

a bottleneck of evolution
sewn together with sinew and string,
a project of total fiction.

The many-voiced powers of song
toe the line between irony and piety,
an intimation of divine retribution

at the point where ice meets water.
The machine version of death
is the forgotten language of light.

The opposite of the body is the world.
Here come the young and digital;
sleep is running away from the clock.

The Secret Life of the Artist
for Kate

Riding the wing of rapture
through nightlong dreams,

flameproof angels collude
with blood and flesh and time.

In the mountains of memory
wolves howl their luetic songs;

in disremembered moments
hoof and hide combust, hair

becomes wing, becomes brush.
Painted wounds open then heal.

•

The past is a journal, a process,
lines hidden under new colours,

possibilities of implication asking
if we are willing to be touched.

So many secrets, so many marks
obliterated. You don't like being

human; the horse gives itself
to the rider, the generous heart

gives birth. All is of the body,
which remembers and cannot lie.

•

Lucid dreaming   animal witness
intimate moments   decoded sound

musical spirits   evoked and invoked
aids to survival   the natural world

I am blessed with torment   an impulse to pray
I draw out of intimacy   find my own way

spirits surround us   companions   assurance
it is all about others   light in the woods

I seek out reflection   offer shared experience
trust the unconscious   Trauma departs

•

How the paintings have changed. I clear
away preconceptions, begin to start again,

to renew conversation after all this time.
Goldfish memory has swum away to be

refined, defined, created in new light,
in the moment of arrival or departure.

The woman in the window does not see
me drive away. Her gaze is in the hand,

the way shadows draw on paper, how
shellac glistens and runs: dictated dreams.

Some Things Just Happen

Speech makes no difference.
Missing documents or silence,
absence makes the heart go find her.
Only that is the present tense.

Leave the domain of the feasible
and crease life's edges well.
If I could do a perfect backflip
the seconds would feel like hours,

words would suddenly come alive,
active participants in creation;
the poem swallow the shadow
on demand each summer morning.

A Table of Moveable Feasts

I am catching a logic bus to coherence,
must protect my anonymous sources.

Negotiated text is mere punctuation,
shadow crosses ghosted on the wall.

The world is full of snapshots
outlined with magic marker.

A dead community is a dead commodity
pointing to us and our fractured state.

Chaos and controversy foreground ephemera
but often open up new doors and concepts.

Getting closer and closer but never arriving
is what this Easter is all about.

•

*Find the Sunday letter for the Year
in the uppermost Line,
and the Golden Number, or Prime,
in the Column of Golden Numbers*

*and against the Prime in the same Line
under the Sunday letter,
you have the Day of the Month
on which Easter falleth that year.*

*Note, that the Name of the Month is set
on the Left Hand, or just within the Figure,
and followeth not, as in other Tables,
by Descent, but by Collateral.*

They be neither dark nor dumb Ceremonies,
but are so set forth, that every man
may understand what they do mean,
and to what use they do serve.

•

In the hotwire delta, ideas come thick
and fast, channelled through postmodern
artists, angels playing in the yard,
and children transfixed by television.

If that was 'snakes on a plane' then what
are these? Twine in sardine cans?
Rubber bands in drawer corners?
Dam the creek, its tributaries!

There are high tides both ends of today
and only office hours inbetween.
I thought of this poem as a way
to use them, to note the change

from purple to brown, to catch up with myself,
then get ahead. But the paintings make
less and less sense, these antique words
seem reactionary and old. *I am become*

like a bottle in the smoke. I made haste
and prolonged not the time. I am small
and of no reputation. I go hence like
the shadow that departed. I am afraid.

The Unbelievable Truth

'The world is full of snapshots representing a vast archive
of untold things, suggesting innumerable histories whispering . . .'
  —Mark Alice Durant, 'The Material in Question',
    in *Marco Bruer. Early Recordings*

Songs, ideas we knew, keep coming back into view,
bobbing up from forgotten pasts like internet friends
from school. Do we know anything about each other
any more? Why does music do what it does, squeeze
memories, emotions out of us all? These endless drones
and synthesizer songs are time machines, black holes

of childhood or despair. I am under their spell, become
enchanted, have no compassion for myself: my building
is on fire. In the strategy room, the aerial wilderness is
crisscrossed with pins and string: the future is not a given.
Unleash the horses now; scrap civilization, career advice
and sleep a little while. The fugitives have won, vultures

circle. I am six pounds of dynamite impatient for my fuse
to be lit, am far too young to die. Past and language have
not done with me yet, I must dance into the goodbye land.
Nobody's perfect, although the cyclops can see more clearly
than most what's wrong with the world. Unfocused moments
sail by: we are rotten fodder for the future, who stay hungry

and still do wrong. Thanks for sending me this music,
echo, tremolo and delay. Everything means something,
nothing means everything. All I understand is that you
don't understand. The unbelievable truth is not easy
to comprehend. I am closing down my house and
getting ready to leave, will take the maps and run.

Understudy

I am buying my way out of poverty and
will show you how far the rabbit hole goes.
Trust me, it is the last night on earth again
and if nothing else I am looking forward.
Everything is surplus over the summer
although I am glad I bought new shoes.

Storms are shredding the season apart,
flood waters continue to rise. We had
to pull over and wait for the rain to stop,
it was so bad on the road. Speak no more
about leaves or grass or the idea of us
going camping. Piled up in my room

are new books and CDs which no-one wants
to review. I am not surprised. Who cares
what we read or listen to, what anyone
thinks about these things? What does it matter
if markets crash or yobs take over the world?
I long for time alone, retreat again to my hole.

Underground, there is a faint echo of above.
We all have friends on facebook and email
each other for company. We are not homesick
and do not need to know what is going on.
Watery stars and fragments of winter
have ruined the summer, blown us into

the information age. Above and beyond us,
just out of sight, is the field of action.
Spend at the sales to save yourself money
as long as your credit rating stays high.
In this scheme of things, whatever the weather,
the whole earth receives a new blessing.

What You Are, the World Is

The time, the self, the frame, the eraser.
Shapes and shadows, the margins as centre;
dark pictures the sum of their parts.

Collaborative drawings, figures in motion,
uncanny perceptions, fortunate objects:
primeval systems after the fall,

dune formations along the dixie highway:
footprints and other signs of life.
The world is full of objects, interruptions,

killing machines and other stories.
All my friends are dead on the ground.
Above the cloud, you feel like an angel.

When the Crowds Have Gone
for Billy Jenkins

When the crowds have gone
the music and musician remain.
Their conversation has ended—
they stand together in silence.

When this room fills with afternoon sun
it remembers me, reads my books
and sniffs my dreams. Your CD
was playing when I came in.

When your guitar moans aloud
and the speakers start to shake
it's as though you've popped round
because you have something to say.

It's all blues now. This house
may be made with walls of noise,
but it wasn't built to last.
We're all strangers now.

You wouldn't be impressed
by our friendly neighbourhood;
we're a company of dusty moths
circling dull suburban dreams.

When the children have gone
the lollipop lady slopes off
with only one or two thankyous
for company at dinner time.

When the children have gone to bed
we remember who we used to be
and what the music was for
before we stopped listening.

If you find the crumpled photo
I discarded on the beach,
bury it for me; build a castle
and give it to the tide to keep.

If you find a way to capture rain
then will you send me some?
If you can, slow right down.
Send me a sign if not a song.

When you take the air away
everything breathes in then out
to make sure we're still alive.
It's often impossible to know.

When the crowds have gone
when money's really tight
when everything's too fast
when you cry till your eyes are red
when you've sucked the poison out
when you don't come round and see me anymore
the handmade music remains.

Days for Amnesiacs

Days for Amnesiacs

Days you were learning to walk and we went around the block each morning, visiting the fountain, the poodle and the old lady who waved at you through the window.

Days before you could walk and I pushed the buggy into town.

Days of cold sunshine.

Days I'd rather stay at home.

Days learning to sail in Norfolk, the slow tacking of wooden boats.

Days teaching sailing on the Norfolk Broads.

Days on the creek, paddling kayaks in the sun.

Days wished away.

Days spent reading.

Days spent wishing I could spend reading.

Days listening to music.

Days downloading music.

Days that disappear before they start.

Days I wish I could spend with you.

Days I'd like to be alone.

Days in Manhattan, walking the streets, visiting museums, galleries and bars.

Days feeling homesick.

Days wondering where home is any more.

Days when it doesn't stop raining.

Days when the cats slept in front of the fire all day.

Days in Italy, warm right through.

Days of painted angels and bible stories, visions and visitations.

Days I'd rather forget.

Days I can't recall.

Days when I want to be quiet and alone.

Days that last for ever.

Days that lasted for ever.

Days of overheard conversations and poignant remarks.

Days when the words insist on making themselves known but resist a sense of order.

Days when light falls on objects.

Days when form imposes itself.

Days when I am disinterested.

Days of rituals and systems, the right way to do things.

Days of interjections and asides.

Days when only Bob Dylan will do.

Days when the headlines don't make sense.

Days when I'd rather just stay in bed.

Days of celebration.

Days of senseless argument.

Days when I forget who I am supposed to be.

Days stretching ahead toward old age.

Days when I miss my friends.

Days spent cycling around the alleys and the park.

Days when I was late home from school.

Days when I just want to scream.

Days when things hide in the shadows.

Days when I just can't be bothered.

Days when I wonder what we're doing here.

Days when I wouldn't live anywhere else.

Days when words don't make any sense.

Days when everything makes me cry.

Days when I can't wait to go to sleep.

Days when the music drifts by as background noise.

Days when you want to dance.

Days when the television stays on too much.

Days before Christmas when I'm just not in the mood.

Days when the garden is full of flowers.

Days when we eat out.

Days spent looking out of the classroom at the river outside.

Days of confusion and doubt.

Days of nervous parenting.

Days when free jazz sounds like noise.

Days when only Anthony Braxton will do, days when Sun Ra is the one.

Days spent filling and stacking boxes, deciding what to keep and what to lose.

Days living in an empty house.

Days at work.

Days when I don't want to be where I am supposed to be.

Days when I'm mean and moody.

Days when I am the luckiest man alive.

Days for Amnesiacs 2

Days when my father was alive.

Days when he took me to school.

Days when he refereed school football matches and drove the whole team there in his Triumph Herald estate.

Days when I played rugby.

Days spent poring over album sleeves and lyrics, days of endless music.

Days in London pubs and clubs watching bands, some of whom went on to become famous.

Days we played ball in the park and went on the swings.

Days Brian later wrote about in a novel.

Days at school I was nostalgic about until I went to a class reunion twenty years on.

Days when mum would start hoovering the house and disappear, to be found later reading in a bedroom or on the stairs.

Days cycling in the sunshine, perhaps to the park, or along the towpath; sometimes further out of town.

Days painting scenery for school plays.

Days when guilt and confession hung over every hour of lessons.

Days which ended at lunchtime, half-day holidays spent riding buses or playing wargames.

Days spent talking to Tim by the river.

Days spent driving to my aunt and uncles, now only a two hour trip.

Days spent driving to Devon, which now only takes four hours.

Days wondering why it's so far from Cornwall to London.

Days wondering about girls.

Days worrying about girls.

Days spent longing and lusting.

Days in love.

Days of the longest holiday summer ever, when O levels finished and there was nothing to do until September.

Days debating whether to go to art college or stay in the sixth form.

Days spent life drawing, trying to balance the three very different systems we were taught.

Days spent watching old Pink Floyd tapes in the video studio.

Days when bus drivers were on strike or my motorbike broke down and you collected me in the car.

Days which started at 6am with my paper round.

Days when grandma wouldn't talk to me because I had a perm.

Days cycling down to visit her.

Days not knowing how long you were going to live.

Days not knowing when you were going to die.

Days for Amnesiacs 3

Days when the tide and wind conspire against canoeing.

Days when the children make it impossible to think or write.

Days when you save things as they are sure to come in useful.

Days when what you thought would be useful isn't.

Days when you can't sleep.

Days when all you can do is sleep.

Days when there is something there, just out sight.

Days when writing makes the children impossible.

Days when talking makes no sense.

Days when you are grounded.

Days when the pile of unread books hold all sorts of future delight.

Days when the pile of unread books is a siren you desire.

Days when you wonder how you are ever going to read it all.

Days when talking is nonsense.

Days when you don't really want to open your eyes or ever breathe again.

Days when it rains and you wonder why on earth you moved house.

Days when you walk by the creek to remind yourself why you live here.

Days when friends arrive unannounced and the sun comes out.

Days when everyone is sailing and canoeing and you hold impromptu picnics.

Days when you camp in the garden.

Days when I run out of words to write.

OCTOBER'S LANGUAGE

for Alan, Hamish, Kingsley, Larry, Martin,
Peter, Richard, Tim and Oliver—
friends old and new

STRANGE OVERTONES

It is the earliest work we revisit most,
whenever it's on display. Nobody eats
in the pub anymore since you went away.

The secret to quiet is to not think about it.
If you let noise in then life takes up the pulse
and your turning circle immediately shrinks

as every particle's energised and shakes itself
awake. I have copied the music you wanted
but have not got an address to send it to.

The guitar has detuned nicely, I am surprised
each time I try to play. I like the concept
of unprepared music now I've thought of it.

No more songs: life is long and I have had
my fill. I ain't never giving in but there aren't
enough hours left in the day, or days until I die.

In the road movie of my life I am parked up,
watching the cars go by, trying to remember
the earth is a flower and that nobody wants

a lonely heart. I am in the habit of silence,
of closing my eyes during sleep, but now
it has been suggested that love comes back

to try again if only we stay awake at all times,
stride out of the dreamtime into the image
of the one, with eyes in focus and mind at rest,

ready to be broken and then mended. I make do
with rests and catnaps, your bruised and smeared
self-portraits green and purple in my mind.

Up for Review

A rough summary is available, but you can click here
for a bigger image, however surprised you are
to see the name of that particular author at the end

of yesterday's newspaper article. There are piles
of my books everywhere, organised by subjects
I might have to teach, depending on how the review

goes in a few weeks time. Meanwhile, two publishers
consider the relationship between public demand
and personal interest in words I wrote a while ago

and am asking them to send out into the world
in a cover of their choice. Rumours of his past
have been exaggerated, and now in addition to

all those unreleased albums there are claims of infidelity
and an unacknowledged son. He is not here to speak
up for himself so everybody else will take a turn.

It was long ago and lying seems as easy as lying
seems to be to those inclined to do it. Why do we
do the things we do and how do we go about it?

What preconceptions do we have, what skills could
we bring to radical reorganization? I didn't realise
you deserved a triple CD set; the one I ordered

has not arrived and the record company say that
it's my problem anyway. It's good to know where I stand
in the scheme of things, to be sure it's money wasted.

I'd phone a friend but they're all in mourning or the throes
of separation, else en route to the ECT suite, denying that
they're insane. Are you mad? Are you mad? Are you mad?

Or is it just uncertainty and overload, a long slow drive
through the sleeplog of confusion and dreams?
Who decides? On our first meeting we hit it off so well

but jobs and families have intervened since then.
Only copied music makes a regular journey from here
to where you live. My crawling heart suggests that

I am way too serious, should turn life on it's head
and read the small print which is there for our own good,
but I have an urge for going out among the stars,

along highways like veins that map out possible futures
and imaginary worlds. It seems that I am proper blessed
and unlikely to sell many books. Some things never change.

This is Where You End
for James

Cheap factory sorrow, produced on demand.
'Quilting and pillows,' insists my three year old
in the Rothko room, 'quilting and pillows.'

But I see blood, a long corridor into despair
where processions often take place
and there is a concentration to brightness.

At the end of the line a smudge of light,
reports of tunnels and angel choirs singing.
Shadow catchers wait to break your fall

and steal your dreams, the paintings
did not impress. The colour itself
has not stayed true, is now a different hue,

and it is impossible to date the language
or intent. Constant negotiation is required
to disrupt mystery and focus on the current show.

Listening again to the past it is clear the boys
were ahead of themselves and deserve to be
revisited. Broken writing and remixed tracks

do not do them justice, are just lost sensations
glimpsed across the room. The music has
an urge for going, was last seen over there;

today it is the sound of now, stumbling awkwardly
as time pauses or pools away. I try to remember
the tiniest of moments, the sudden unkempt tunes

you played in the living room. I could be doing
something else but the landscape has changed
just as I have gone to ground in a place

you never knew, where monotone rain is broken
only by squares of painted colour on the wall
and tiny echoes from my personal stereo.

Borrowed Time

In the spring I sometimes felt like getting up early
and painting, tweaking a poem or two into shape
over a cup of coffee, then making toast for everyone

at the normal time. Now, I'm claiming back the hour
that someone borrowed, soon it will be dark before
I drive home from work. I'm not a mirror to myself,

but sometimes I know just how I feel. I've run out
of words and inclinations, wonder what on earth
I am doing here. Nothing ever seems quite right

and my little girl has to like it or lump it: stay with
her friends or branch out on her own at another
local school. As recession bites, we change our tune

and learn to sing for our supper. The pub is full
of strangers doing the quiz we didn't want to enter;
seems we've got the question wrong and don't

understand the given answer. I turn over and over
in my mind this outmoded style of living,
the relationship between ourselves and others.

There is no place here for simile or metaphor, we must
exploit the intimacy between experience and self.
You would be forgiven for thinking I didn't exist at all.

How We Came to Be Where We Are
a found poem

Words are composed of layered compositions,
looping organic outlines of monochrome shapes
at once non-representational and oddly familiar,

figures full of curves, rounded lines and slithering
forms. They suggest visual movement and states
of continual change. One thinks of the shifting

shapes of clouds in the sky, the ever elongating
and truncating gyrations of mysterious goo
in a lava lamp. One thinks of blue moods,

blue highways, blue notes, blue movies,
even blue states. Blue tends to be associated
with more contemplative states of mind;

these words bring together sight and sound
in a celebration of the freedom that comes
through modulations of order, gesture and

graphic clarity, as one musical motif folds
into another, inspired by the interplay of
metaphor adapted from found text.

Stories All Around Us

Having previously forgotten I now choose
to remember. Poetry is not the answer
nor is interrogating the text you wanted

me to read. New students are talking outside,
in here my class are learning to write to order
and make sense of incoherent instructions.

It is not as easy as falling off a bike,
it is more like chewing on a cloud:
there's nothing there, just wisps of thought

and dream, songs that won't go away.
The ego & the id, superman or chosen procedure:
life is up for grabs if only you remember

to switch off the light as you leave. A door
slams behind me. I want to make more sense
but in the dark it's difficult to see.

What am I attempting to define? If we cling
to the essence, we will come to no harm,
but it does not make the advice universal

or it easier to police the distance
between forward and backward motion.
The landscape has not changed and

this is not a manifesto for waiting.
In the human mind's vast reservoir
something as well as nothing has happened.

Unwanted Visitors

Tonight, an old friend phoned to say
that he had separated, twenty five years on,
from the girl he met through me.

Said only that, in clipped business tone,
assuring me it had all been worked out
a year ago and that nobody was hurt.

I don't believe a word but didn't know
what to say. Later, tears arrived.
A mutual friend was shocked that it

was left to me to break the news.
Meanwhile, my daughter fences air
and follows instructions, warming up

in a circuit round the gym. Everything
turns out to be true, the pictures prove it.
We never doubted or voiced our suspicions

about the past offered to us in the pub,
but when I got home I found your friend
curled foetal on the table, fast asleep,

having somehow managed to let himself in.
Earlier, the post office had no stamps
and was about to shut for good.

Last week the postmistress was in tears,
today she's all smiles in a dark suit,
busy taking photos of her last customers,

wanting to remember years of work
before they all get thrown away.
Tomorrow, I will have to drive

to buy my stamps, and the village
will have shrunk to houses, church
and pub. Change has let itself in again

and instead of wherever it is we are,
we will all be somewhere else. You can't
do anything until it starts to happen

and then you're powerless anyway.
Someone waves goodbye and walks
out of your life, leaving not a whisper.

A Few Thoughts About Blogging

I got to thinking that perhaps I'd got it wrong
and that we all disagreed about fundamental things.
Who could or would write this? How could we

be any more ignored? I diffused the argument
by justifying all your perverse decisions
and offering myself cut flowers. The world

has changed and we can never know everything.
Meeting places and traditional pubs are thin
on the ground, but who is to say that shouting

out loud doesn't work, or that someone might
notice us even as they look right through us?
Invisibility and self-deprecation are certainly

useful assets to have, and there is something
to be said for the sieving effect of time
but I don't like the idea of counting numbers

or keeping my work locked in the drawer.
Commuter anthems are no longer a reflection
of cultural time and space, just a way

to pass the time as we drive to work each day.
The mark on the bench can be read as a benchmark,
to which we all refer. Meanwhile, I'll continue

to steam envelopes open, hoping for money inside,
looking for mutal attraction and letting myself off
the hook. Love's a disease—why do we need

to read this stuff or roll the credits every time?
I still have the girls, that's the way boys are.
It's obvious to me that this is where you end,

that afterglow and sunburst collide in your heart.
The tree with lights in it isn't up yet, but this year
we should plan well ahead, write a field guide

to confession and how to greet the little gods
who post these inconsistent pages and never
apologise for their lack of principles or dreams.

Fractured then gathered, with nothing substantial
to have or to hold; a little bit of alternative history
makes us feel we're not the only weirdos around.

I've said it before and I'll say it again, who could
or would write this? How could we be any more ignored?
Is this truly wonderland or just a paperless machine?

Be Serious

It's easy being right on, harder working hard
when you'd rather be at home, growing up
late and trying to stay alive. Outside,

the roads go to you and where we used
to live. Now there is only endless scenery
and a wish for something more. I lay

my ear to the furious night and watch you
breathe and sleep. I never lose, not really,
am ready for October's language to fall

into place. Doors open the other way
as harvest is taken home. I'm still
waiting for an intelligent response.

The Last Word from Paradise

There is nothing to be frightened of.
I could write this in fire, point out
that exile is a mapless geometry,

a short life of trouble in the library
of dust before uncertain alchemy
and a procession of constructed drift.

At the heart of this cheery reading
are stark images from the archive,
fake letters to the editor from those who

have no truck with established thinking
on the subject. The present alone is
our happiness, the balance between then

and becoming. It is easier not to think,
to memorize concern and understanding.
Competing visions pose a threat,

associations are often rapid and musical.
What is there to believe in? How can you
ask me that? It is obvious that there is

a wider social and artistic context,
no reason to despair. Every individual
is the author of their own repair.

Do You Ever Get Lonely?

Good question. If I wasn't talking
to you, I probably would. But I am.
The rain has suddenly eased,

it's been drumming on the roof
for best part of an hour. I'm
supposed to be elsewhere right now,

answering questions about nothing
in particular, but I can hardly see
through the pockmarked windscreen.

You've been gone for several days
and I still can't get used to driving
the other car. You phoned to say

the snow had settled, that there was
no power to your parents' house.
The kids were still awake, they

don't believe you that it's dark
when you shut your eyes. Well,
they kind of know it but they don't.

Maybe we pampered them when
they were young, perhaps they just
like light? Either way, there are

no more questions to be asked.
If I were you I'd be lonelier still.
And if you were me? You're not,

so let that be the end of that.
My job seems to be disappearing fast,
creative writing written out

of the equation. New maps and plans
proliferate, I trace obsessive forms
and count the days still left to go.

Ephemera piles up, along with
further attempts to understand these
moments of indecision and delay.

In Everything Give Thanks

The man who does not exist
keeps sending me books and records.
The letterbox is full of well meaning

poems that seem to feature me,
and CDs of bands I've never heard of.
In momentary breaks, opportunities

arise and nothing has happened yet.
It is always a surprise, that moment
of recognition and engagement,

the startling noise of caterwaul
or electronic fidget. Do you know
the story of the boy on a ladder

and what he climbed to see? No,
neither do I, but I would like to.
When you left I found your watch

and several empty wine bottles,
words we spoke last night still
circling, loud music in my head.

The things you do not know
are an opportunity for me to send
the wrong object, or hold forth

in drunken erudition. I am the king
of thieves when it comes to culture,
and you'll miss me when you're gone.

Sources

'The House with the Red Door': letter from Clark Allison; *Views from a Tuft of Grass*, Harry Martinson; *Real Cities*, Steve Pile | 'A Wing & a Prayer': *Artificial Illuminations*, Olivo Barbieri; *A Passage Through Silence and Light*, Hélène Binet; *Boyd & Evans* (2007 catalogue); *Another Future*, Alan Gilbert; *The Letters of Ted Hughes*; *A Nomad Poetics*, Pierre Joris; *Today I Wrote Nothing*, Daniil Kharms; *Sprawling Places*, David Kolb; *Bits of Wood*, Will Menter; *The Architect's Brother*, Robert ParkeHarrison; *On Listening*, Fiona Sampson; *Bunker*, Erasmus Schröter; *secret notebook.wild pages* blog; *Short Fiction*, issue 1; Song titles by Algebra Suicide, James Blackshaw, Doug Burr, Cheer, Adele Diane, Dyzan, Dirtmusic, Guillemots, Laura Marling, Marilyn Mazur & Jan Garbarek, Reuben Radding, Kimmie Rhodes, Schleimer K, Richard Shindell, Suishou No Fune, White Hinterland, Chris Wood, and on the anthology *John Barleycorn Reborn*; 'Piece by Piece, Artists' Hands Made a Home', Joyce Wadler in *The New York Times*, March 2008 | 'A Collection of Relics': *Witkin*, Germano Celant; *Ralph Eugene Meatyard*, ed. James Baker Hall; *Ralph Eugene Meatyard. An American Vision*, ed Barbara Tannernbaum | 'Conviction': heavenlyhouseboatblues.blogspot.com | 'Forgotten Outposts': *Phantom Channel Compilation*; 'Thomas Nozkowski at Fisher Landau', *Gusto*, April 06 2008 | Fugitive Scripting': *Night Haunts*, Sukhdev Sandhu; *Iain Sinclair*, Robert Sheppard | 'A Glance is Enough': *Looking at Sean Scully's Painting*, Hood Museum of Art; *Sean Scully. The Art of the Stripe*, Hood Museum of Art; *The Quakers. A Very Short Introduction*, Pink Dandelion; *As Easy as Lying*, H.L. Hix; *A Nomad Poetics*, Pierre Joris; *Today I Wrote Nothing*, Daniil Kharms; *On Listening*, Fiona Sampson | 'Going Under': song titles by Centro-matic, Eluvium, Ben Frost, Richard Garet, Stina Nordenstom, The Wolfgang Press | 'Intermittent': poems by Peter Dent | 'The Museum of Lists': *Artforum*, March 2008; *Today I Wrote Nothing*, Daniil Kharms; *On Listening*, Fiona Sampson | 'Questions on Form': *On Form*, Angela Leighton; *A Defense of Ardor*, Adam Zagajewski | 'The Secret Life of the Artist': 'Outside In: an interview with Greg Bottoms'; 'Travels with My Mom' in *LRB* August 2007, Terry Castle; 'From Genesis to Ennervation', Richard Cook review of *Dreams Less Sweet* | 'Some Things Just Happen': *Art Review*, #11, May 2007; 'i hate scotland', Ballboy; *Science Fiction*, Roger Luckhurst; *Polish Writers on Writing*, ed. Adam Zagajewski | 'A Table of Moveable Feasts': *The Book of Common Prayer*; Bob Garlitz blog | 'The Unbelievable Truth': song titles by Centro-matic, Elton Dean, Talking Heads, Jimi Tenor, Toe, Will Johnson and Prefuse 73 | 'What You Are, the World Is': *Artforum. Best of 2007*, December 2007 | 'How We Came to Be Where We Are': Eleanor Heartney, invitation card for Viktor Kord's 'Algorithm and Blues. New Paintings', June Kelly Gallery NYC 2008.

www.ingramcontent.com/pod-product-compliance
Lightning Source LLC
Chambersburg PA
CBHW021327190426
43193CB00039B/413